MESILA
Providing The Path to Financial Stability

AF882110

MESILA JUNIOR HIGH SCHOOL PROGRAM

Student Workbook

Sephardic Yeshiva Version

Student Workbook - Sephardic Yeshiva Version

© 2017
All rights reserved.
No part of this guide may be reproduced in any form or by any means
without prior written permission from Mesila.

ISBN 978-1-941902-30-1

Please note:

This material is intended for use exclusively in the context of a Mesila-authorized course.
It may not be used without prior written permission from Mesila's Jerusalem headquarters.

MESILA
Providing The Path to Financial Stability

Questions or comments may be sent to:

Mesila

P.O.B. 57116 Jerusalem 9157002, Israel
Tel: +972.2.500.0475 • Fax: +972.2.500.0478
info@mesila.org • www.mesila.org
Reg. Amuta No. 580361236

Mesila USA

POB 838 Monsey NY 10952
Tel: 212.784.6780
info@mesilausa.org
www.mesilausa.org

Mesila UK

Tel: 333 344 1711
info@mesilauk.org • www.mesilauk.org
Reg. Charity No. 1114573

Table of Contents

Dear Student,

Mesila is an organization that helps people of all ages learn how to use their money in a smart, responsible way, so that money shouldn't be a cause of stress, strife, or misery.

We're supposed to use our money to do good things – to take care of ourselves and our families, to help others, and to enable Torah learning. But we can only do that if we are in control of our money, and we don't let money control us.

People often think that if they only had more money, many of their problems would be solved. But the truth is that the key to avoiding financial problems is not having a lot of money, but using your money wisely.

The purpose of this program is to help you learn how to use money the way Hashem intended, and develop healthy financial habits that will stay with you for the rest of your life, b'ezrat Hashem. Whether you have a lot of money or a little, knowing what to do with it – and what not to do with it – will help you to achieve great things.

Sincerely,

Mesila

UNIT 1

Introduction: CRASH COURSE IN ECONOMICS

A long time ago, all of the Jewish people lived in Israel, and King David was their king. He was their leader in both spiritual and economic matters, guiding them in Torah and everyday life.

King David had a harp hanging over his bed, and at midnight, the wind blew, and made music from the harp. David, the king, would quickly get up and start learning Torah until morning. One morning, the Sages came to King David and said, "Our master the king! Your people, the Jews, need money!" He said to them, "Go and earn money from each other."

(Based on Gemara Sanhedrin 16a)

WHAT IS MONEY?

Money is a tool with which people get the things they need and want.

There are two kinds of things money can buy: goods and services.

Goods are *objects or products*, such as food, clothing, houses, toys, etc.

Services are things that people or companies do or provide, such as designing, babysitting, haircutting, fixing, etc.

People **pay** money in exchange for goods and services that they consider valuable.

People **earn** money by providing useful goods or services to others.

Money flowing from one person to another in a way that benefits a chain of people is the basis of an **economy**. An economy is a system in which money is earned and spent by the people of a community or society.

When people provide goods and services for each other, they accomplish several things:

1) They earn money for themselves.
2) They keep money flowing, boosting the health of the economy.
3) They help others, and do chessed with one another.

Hashem blessed each and every person with unique skills and talents that they can use to help others, and in the process earn money for themselves and their family.

It is no coincidence that people get money by helping others and doing chessed. In fact, Hashem's plan for the world was that it should be built and maintained through people doing good things for each other. People may not realize it, but any time they earn money through providing useful goods or services, they are actually doing chessed.

An Economics Lesson From a Great Torah Leader

The world's economy is based on the flow of business. Money has to pass from hand to hand, through thousands of hands, in order to do business, lend money, etc.

"Olam chessed yibaneh - The world is built with kindness" (Tehillim 89:3).

"Why is money called 'zuzim'? Because it moves ["zaz"] from one person to another." (Bamidbar Rabbah 22:7). *The power of money lies in its mobility.*

(Rav Elchonon Wasserman, Ikveta d'Meshicha, p. 8)

Follow the Trail of the $50 Bill

Here's an example of how the flow of money from one hand to another strengthens the economy while helping people at the same time:

A Microeconomic Tale

Gabriel Levi, age 10, really wants his own etrog, and he has an idea of how he can buy his own set: He has an aravot bush in his backyard, and he'll sell aravot outside the synagogue before Succot and use the money to buy the etrog. His mother gives him permission to cut branches from the bush and sell them, and he sells the aravot for $5 a pair. He sells 10 pairs, and earns $50. He puts the $50 bill in his wallet and goes to spend the money on his very own etrog.

Mr. Harari is an etrog dealer. One day before Succot, Gabriel Levi walks into his shop. "I have $50 to spend on an etrog," he says proudly. "Can you show me the nicest etrog you have for that price?"

Mr. Harari helps Gabriel choose a lovely etrog, and places the $50 in his wallet.

Erev Succot, Mrs. Harari looks at her watch and sees that it's already 10:30 in the morning. "Uh oh," she thinks, "my succah still has no lights!" Mr. Harari is still out selling etrogim, and Mrs. Harari doesn't know what to do. She quickly picks up the phone and calls Chaim, the electrician. "Can you come down and set up the lights in my succah?" she pleads.

"Sure," Chaim says. "I'll be right over."

An hour later, the Hararis' succah is bright and cheery, and Mrs. Harari is bright and cheery as well as she pulls out the $50 to pay Chaim.

The $50 safely in his pocket, Chaim the electrician runs over to Levi's Liquor Store just before closing time and buys wine for the Chag. "Great," he thinks. "I was running low on cash, and I didn't know if I'd be able to get the wine I wanted for simchat Chag."

Mr. Levi closes his liquor store and goes home to get ready for the Chag. "Gabriel," he calls, "did you end up buying yourself an etrog?"

"Yes, Abba," Gabriel says excitedly. "Look! Isn't it beautiful?"

"It sure is," says Mr. Levi. "How much was it?"

"Fifty dollars," says Gabriel. "That's what I made selling aravot."

Mr. Levi reaches into his pocket. "I just made one last extra sale as I was closing the store," he says, "and it was exactly $50. Here – I want to pay for your etrog."

The End

Follow the Trail of the $50 Bill

REVIEW

Look how many wonderful things happened through the travels of one $50 bill!

1) How many times did the $50 move from hand to hand? ______________________

2) Rav Elchonon Wasserman writes that "The power of money lies in its mobility." What is the total dollar value of the economic activity that happened because of the movement of the $50 bill from hand to hand?
(***Hint:*** *Economic activity is the total of all the money earned and spent through the flow of money from one person to another.*)

____

3) List the goods and services provided and received through the travels of the $50 bill.

____

____

____

____

____

4) List the mitzvot and acts of chessed that happened as a result of the travels of the $50 bill.

____

____

____

____

____

5) On a separate sheet of paper, write a story (real or fictitious) about another $50 bill, following it along a journey of four or five good deeds.

The Value of Money

A Few Silly Papers

Once upon a time, a Jewish businessman got stranded on a desert island with nothing but his wallet. "At least I have a credit card and cash," he thought to himself. When he finally met an island native, he immediately pulled out a wad of bills and asked, "Where can I buy a can of soda?"

The native stared at the wad of bills. "Me no eat paper," he said.

"No, no," explained the businessman. "I want to buy a drink with this."

"Me no drink paper," said the native.

"Wait a minute," said the businessman. "Haven't you ever seen money before? You can buy things with this. You give this to people, and they give you stuff to eat, stuff to wear, stuff to build – it's fantastic!"

The native eyed him quizzically, as if to say: Why would anyone give something of worth in exchange for a few silly green papers with pictures on them of old men who need haircuts?

Worthless Money

Rav Reuven Dov Dessler, the father of Rav Eliyahu Eliezer Dessler, author of *Michtav Me'Eliyahu*, was a wealthy man. During World War I, when the tides of war turned against the Germans, Rav Reuven Dov changed all of his money from German marks into Russian rubles, thinking that the ruble would be a more stable currency. A short while after the Bolsheviks took power in 1918, the ruble was declared invalid and lost all of its worth. In an instant, Rav Reuven Dov went from being a rich man to a pauper.

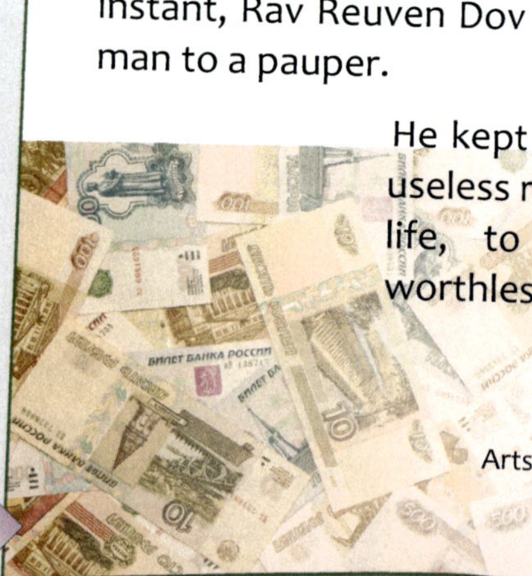

He kept two suitcases of these useless rubles for the rest of his life, to remind himself of the worthlessness of money.

(Based on *Rav Dessler*, by Yonoson Rosenblum, Artscroll/Mesorah, 2000, pp. 92-93)

Understanding that money has no real value can help us understand the Sages' teaching about true wealth (*Pirkei Avot* 4:1): "Who is rich? He who is happy with his portion."

Someone who has a lot of money is not truly *rich*, because his money has no value: he can't eat it, he can't wear it, he can't build a house with it. Only someone who is happy with what he has can truly be considered rich.

UNIT 2

MONEY IN ACTION

Money's Many Identities

Identity #1

THE ATM SPITS IT OUT IN A FLASH,
THEN PEOPLE DASH
TO A SHOPPING BASH
BUT IF YOU USE IT UP, IT'S GONE,
SO DON'T BE RASH.
SAVE IT UP, AND YOU'LL HAVE A STASH.

WHO AM I? ______________

Identity #2

I'M A PIECE OF PAPER,
BUT I'M IN YOUR NAME.
YOU CAN BOUNCE ME,
BUT THAT WOULD BE A SHAME.
YOU CAN MAKE ME OUT TO ANY AMOUNT,
BUT NOT MORE THAN YOU HAVE
IN YOUR ACCOUNT.

WHO AM I? ______________

Identity #3

ON MY BACK, THERE'S A MAGNETIC STRIP,
SWIPE ME, AND I'LL PAY FOR YOUR TRIP.
I CALL MYSELF MASTER,
BUT I'M REALLY JUST A DRAIN.
WHEN YOU PAY THE BILL,
THAT'S WHEN YOU'LL FEEL THE PAIN.

WHO AM I? ______________

WHO AM I?

Instructions: *Each of the statements below describes one (or more) of money's three identities. Fill in the correct form of money after each statement.*

1. You know exactly how much you have. ______________
2. You pay high interest if you pay late. ______________
3. If you spend more than you have in your account, the bank will charge you. ______________
4. If it's lost or stolen, you can stop payment. ______________ ______________

5. If it's lost or stolen, there's nothing you can do. ______________
6. Can be post-dated to delay payment. ______________

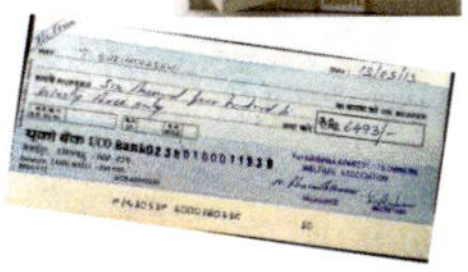

7. You can only pay in person, not by phone, mail, or computer. ______________
8. No fees, hidden costs, or penalties. ______________
9. Gives you points and rewards. ______________
10. You get a clearly itemized monthly statement, so you know how much you spent on what. ______________
11. It might be counterfeit. ______________
12. You don't know how much you spent on what. ______________
13. You don't feel like you're parting with money, so you're likely to spend more than you would otherwise have spent. ______________
14. It's really just a loan. ______________
15. If you use it impulsively, without thinking or planning, you won't be able to use it when you really need it. ______________ ______________ ______________

Financial Shortfalls

What Happens When You Run Out of Money?

Do you recognize this scene?

You're standing at the store's checkout counter, watching the cashier ring up your bill, and you start getting this funny pit in your stomach. As the numbers on the cash register keep going up and up, it occurs to you that this might be a good time to count up exactly how much money you actually have with you. You pull out your wallet, and with a line of people watching from behind you, you pull out one bill, and then another, and then another, and then – that's it! Nervously, you fish through the coin compartment, but after digging out every last penny, something tells you that you have a problem. You look up at the final total on the cash register, and realize that there's no way this is going to work. Whoops! Now what?

Let's face it – every person runs out of money sometimes:

- A kid in a pizza shop
- A parent on Erev Yom Tov
- A businessman who runs into extra expenses
- A *bachur* in yeshiva who uses up his monthly allowance

What happens if you don't have enough money to buy what you want at the time when you want to buy it?

It happens to all of us. It's normal. It doesn't necessarily mean you're poor, and it's not a reason to panic. But different people react differently to this situation. And not all reactions are created equal. Here are five typical reactions to the very common predicament of not having money:

Sandy Schnorrer

"My friends always have extra money on them. When I run out – and I always do – I just ask them for more. It's usually just a little bit."

Barry Borrower

"Can you lend me a few dollars? I'll pay you back as soon as I can. I know I owe you money from last time, but I really need it. Pretty please?"

Pat Planner

"I knew I was going to need money, so I made sure to line up jobs raking leaves every night this week so I would have what I needed."

Calvin Coper

"I ran out of money, so I'm not going to spend until I get more. And you know what? It's no great tragedy."

Scott Saver

"Every time I get a dollar, I make sure to put fifty cents in my money jar, and I put the jar up on a high shelf so my little brother shouldn't get his hands on it. When I run out of money, and there's something I really want, I just dip into my trusty jar."

Scott Says...

A Lesson on Borrowing

1. Scott Saver and Barry Borrower both want the same pair of $60 sneakers. Barry runs to all his friends to see what kind of loans he can drum up, and rushes to buy the sneakers. At the store, he bumps into Scott Saver, who pulls out his wallet and pays for the sneakers with the money he saved up. Six months later, when the sneakers are all beat up, Barry is still worrying about how to pay back all his debts, while Scott is busy saving up for his next pair. "Savings are a loan to yourself," Scott says.

   EXPLAIN WHAT SCOTT MEANS. ______________________________

   ____

   ____

   ____

2. Eventually, Barry Borrower's friends get sick of lending him money. So he goes out and gets himself a credit card. "It's a great thing," he tells his friend Scott. "I don't need to borrow anymore. I never run out of money."
   "That's what you think," Scott says. "A credit card is just a fancy way of borrowing – and you might have to pay lots of interest, too."

   EXPLAIN WHAT SCOTT MEANS. ______________________________

   ____

   ____

   ____

3. One day, Scott Saver meets Barry Borrower riding a spanking new bike. "Nice bike, Barry," he says.
   "I know what you're thinking, Scott," Barry says. "And this time, you're wrong! I didn't borrow a penny to buy this bike! I took out an installment plan, and I only have to pay $10 a month for the next 18 months.'
   "Bad deal, Barry," Scott says. "I'm saving up for the same bike, but it's only going to cost me $140. And besides, you may not have borrowed from me, but you did borrow from the store."

   A) EXPLAIN WHAT SCOTT MEANS WHEN HE SAYS THAT BARRY DID A BAD DEAL. ______________________________

   ____

   ____

   ____

   B) EXPLAIN WHAT SCOTT MEANS WHEN HE SAYS THAT BARRY BORROWED FROM THE STORE.

   ____

   ____

   ____

וְנָא אַל תַּצְרִיכֵנוּ ה' אֱלֹקֵינוּ לֹא לִידֵי מַתְּנַת בָּשָׂר וָדָם וְלֹא לִידֵי הַלְוָאָתָם. (ברכת המזון)

Please, Hashem, do not make us needy of the gifts of people or of their loans. (Birkat HaMazon)

Pat's Plans

A Lesson in Entrepreneurship

PAT PLANNER AND HIS FRIEND CALVIN COPER ARE DREAMING OF TAKING A TRIP TO ERETZ YISRAEL FOR SUCCOT, BUT NEITHER ONE HAS THE MONEY FOR A TICKET.

PAT DECIDES THAT HE'S GOING TO EARN THE MONEY TO PAY FOR HIS TRIP TO ERETZ YISRAEL. THESE ARE THE STEPS HE FOLLOWS:

Step 1: Finding a need that you can fill

"In order to make money," Pat says, "I'll have to think about what people in my neighborhood need that I can provide. There's no tutoring program for the kids in my area, who stay in the city in the summer. I'm a good student and I'm great with kids. It's all about supply and demand – there's a demand for a tutoring program, and if I can supply it, then I'm in business."

Step 2: Market research

"But how do I know that people will want to send their kids to my tutoring program?" Pat wonders. "I better speak to the parents in the area and find out. I also need to find out what the going prices are for tutoring by a teenager in other parts of the neighborhood."

Step 3: Pricing

"Let's see," says Pat. "I'm hoping to earn at least $1,200 this summer to cover my ticket.
How's this going to work?

Considerations:

A. Cost of running a 3-week tutoring program – 5 nights a week:

Renting space in a shul 3 hours a night for 3 weeks: $400
Treats/ prizes: $40 a child (fluctuating expense, depending on number of children)
Advertising: $80 (one-time expense)
Assistant tutor: $620 (fixed expense)

B. Breakeven point:

Option 1:

If I charge each student $150, ($10 an hour per student in each group, 1 hour a night, 5 nights a week) I'll need to have 10 kids in my tutoring program just to cover my expenses and break even. After that, each additional kid will represent $110 in profit.

MESILA
Providing The Path to Financial Stability

Pat's Plans cont'd

That means that if I charge $150, my breakeven point is 10 kids, or $1500.
10 x $40 (cost per student) + $400 (rent) + $620 (assistant) +$80 (advertising) = $1500

Option 2:
If I charge each student $225, ($15 an hour per student in each group, 1 hour a night, 5 nights a week) I'll need to have just 6 kids in my tutoring program to cover my expenses and break even. After that, each additional kid will represent $185 in profit.
That means that if I charge $225, my breakeven point is 6 kids, or $1350:
6 x $40 (cost per kid) + $400 (rent) + $620 (assistant) + $80 (advertising) = $1340 (with $10 to spare)

C. Profit:

In order to save up $1200 for my trip, I need to earn $1200 more than my breakeven point. That means that:
If I charge $150 per kid, I'll need 21 kids in my tutoring program: 10 to break even, and another 11 to profit.

Total revenue: 21 x $150 = $3150
Total expenses: 21 x $40 + $400 + $620 + $80 = $1940
Profit: $3150 - $1940 = $1210

If I charge $225 per kid, I'll need 13 kids in my tutoring program: 6 to break even, and another 7 to profit.

Total revenue: 13 x $225 = $2925
Total expenses: 13 x $40 + $400 + $620 + $80 = $1620
Profit: $2925 - $1620 = $1305

D. Pricing:

"The other tutoring programs in the neighborhood are charging between $180 and $300 for the three-week period," says Pat. "It would be nice to charge less than everyone else, but I don't think it's realistic for me to get the 21 kids I need in order to pay for my ticket, and I wouldn't have enough hours in the evening to teach them either. So I think I'll charge $225, and aim to get at least 15 kids: 6 to break even, another 7 to profit, and another 2 to cover maaser and unexpected expenses. If I get fewer kids than that, it's not worth opening."

Step 4: Marketing

"Now it's time to get the word out," says Pat Planner. "We're going to run a three-pronged campaign: posters, phone calls and advertisements." He prints up signs and hangs them all around, and puts an ad into the local advertising circular. Then he starts making phone calls – not just to the parents in the area, but to anyone he knows. "It's called networking," Pat says. "The more people who know about my tutoring program, the more customers I'll have."

Step 5: Do it - and do it right

"Great," says Pat. "I have 16 kids signed up for my tutoring program. That means I'll even have a bit of extra money to treat them to a fun pizza party at the end – and make sure they'll want to come back next summer. Eretz Yisrael, here I come!"

FIVE CHEERS FOR PAT!

LOOK AT ALL THE GREAT THINGS PAT DID!

1. He earned herself the opportunity to visit Eretz Yisrael.
2. He helped 16 kids catch up with their learning and feel good about themselves.
3. He helped 16 sets of parents give their kids a boost for next year.
4. He gave *maaser* on the money he earned.

AND LAST BUT NOT LEAST:

5. He gave his friend Sammy Schnorrer a job as his assistant so that Sammy would have his own money and wouldn't have to ask others for money anymore. Pat, did you know that giving someone a job is the highest form of tzedakah?

MESILA
Providing The Path to Financial Stability

Class Tzedakah Campaign

Challenge

Your class is going to raise money to donate something that your school needs.

A tzedakah campaign such as this should be built in keeping with the same principles as any business venture. In order to run a successful campaign, therefore, you will need to come up with workable business idea and build a plan for getting the idea off the ground.

STEP 1: FINDING A NEED THAT YOU CAN FILL

Brainstorm – supply and demand:
What products or services are in demand in your community that your class can supply in order to earn money to help your school?

STEP 2: MARKET RESEARCH

Ask your family, neighbors, and friends:

- Would they be willing to pay for the product or service your class is thinking of providing?
- Who else in your community is providing that same product or service?
- Is there room for more people to provide that product or service?
- What is the going rate for what you'd like to provide?

STEP 3: PRICING

Cost

- What type of expenses will you have? (Supplies, advertising, manpower, overhead, etc.)
- How much will each type of expense cost you?
- Which expenses will you have no matter how much you sell (fixed costs)?
- Which expenses will go up the more you sell (fluctuating costs)?

Breakeven point

- How much of your product or service will you have to sell in order to cover just the costs of setting up your venture?

Profit

- How much profit do you need to earn in order to make your venture worthwhile and be able to donate the item your school needs?

Pricing

- How much can you charge for your product or service?
- If you charge more, will you lose customers?
- If you charge less, will you gain customers?
- What is the price that will allow you to bring in the most profit?

STEP 4: MARKETING

Get the word out! Some ways to let people know about your product or service:

- Networking: Tell them, and ask them to tell other people.
- Hang up signs and posters
- Make phone calls
- Advertise in local circulars
- Direct mail

STEP 5: DO IT – AND DO IT RIGHT!

When you provide a product or service, you have to be a professional. That means:

- You keep careful accounts of the money, so that you know exactly how much came in and how much went out. (Otherwise, it is impossible to know how much you've earned.)
- You keep the money of your venture separate from your own money.
- What you do, you do well, without cutting corners.
- You take responsibility for your product or service, and make sure that the customer is satisfied.
- If things go wrong (and they often do), you keep a smile on your face and deal with the situation maturely, without looking to blame others.

HERE ARE SOME IDEAS OF PRODUCTS AND SERVICES YOU CAN PROVIDE IN ORDER TO RAISE MONEY FOR YOUR SCHOOL:

- After-school clubs
- Chanukah/Purim carnival
- Cheesecake for Shavuot
- Cookbook
- Erev Pesach car cleaning service
- Mishloach Manot
- Raffle
- Selling popcorn, lemonade, cholent, etc.
- Tu b'Shvat platters

GOOD LUCK!

MESILA
Providing The Path to Financial Stability

UNIT 3

KIDS' NEEDS AND WANTS

Kids and Stores

Introduction

All people need and want things. Kids often don't have the ability to buy their own stuff, which means that they turn to their parents for what they need or want.

Parents want to give to their children, but sometimes they can't, and sometimes they choose not to, for various reasons (for example, they'll tell you that too much candy is bad for your teeth). As adults with life experience, they understand that love means saying no sometimes.

When you need or want something, what do you do? Let's look at what you *don't* do:

Song:

NEVER TAKE KIDS TO A STORE

Marvelous Midos Machine Volume III, by Abie Rotenberg (used with permission)

I met my good friend Mr. Katz yesterday
He looked all upset, so I started to say
Things can't be so bad, why are you so sad
You better tell me right away

I'd be just as happy as I was before
If only I'd listened and trusted you more
I ignored your advice, now I'm paying the price
I went with all of my kids TO A STORE!

You went to a store with your girls and your boys?
And it was a big store, a store filled with toys
But I warned you not, I know I forgot
Oy it was a day that I did not enjoy

I know just what happened don't tell me a thing
I know 'cause I took my kids there last spring
When you got to the store and walked through the door
All of your kinderlach started to SING:

We want Lego and Construx
And a hockey set deluxe
We want baseballs we want bats
We want helmets we want hats
Like I said to you before, never take kids to a store
All you're gonna hear is, we want more and more

Tatty there's a pretty doll with shiny golden hair
I'm sorry little shayfela am I a millionaire?
You already have that train, I know it works just fine
But look it's such a bargain only $19.99

We want cars and trucks you see
And of course Monopoly
See this camera it's so nice
Look it's made by Fisher Price
Like I said to you before, never take kids to a store
All you're gonna hear is, we want more and more

Why do you need that Care Bear?
There's one at home I think
But Tatty that one's yellow and this one is pink
Do you see this storybook it's something that I need
I'd love to buy it Shmuly,
BUT YOU DON'T KNOW HOW TO READ!

We want robots that can talk
And animals that walk
We want checkers we want chess
WE WON'T EVER LEAVE A MESS!
Like I said to you before, never take kids to a store
All you're gonna hear is, we want more and more

They were crying, they were shouting,
why I'll bet one even screamed
And you whispered, please be quiet,
we don't want to make a scene
So you bought them all they wanted,
more than you can afford
And an hour after you got home, they said....
TATTY WE ARE BORED!

But kids who have good middos,
are simply not that way
They know how to appreciate whatever comes their way
And you can even disregard all that I've said before
And let them come along with you
When - you - go - to - a - store.

Kids and Stores: Review

Questions:

1. WE WANT LEGO AND CONSTRUX
AND A HOCKEY SET DELUXE
WE WANT BASEBALLS WE WANT BATS
WE WANT HELMETS WE WANT HATS.

   Why did these kids suddenly want so much stuff?

   ____

   ____

2. DO YOU SEE THIS STORYBOOK
IT'S SOMETHING THAT I NEED
I'D LOVE TO BUY IT SHMULY,
BUT YOU DON'T KNOW
HOW TO READ!

   Does Shmuly really need the book?
   Why does he think he needs it?

   ____

   ____

3. a) Why would people feel that they need things that don't really need?
   b) Has this ever happened to you?
   c) What made you feel that you needed something you didn't really need?

   ____

   ____

   ____

4. SO YOU BOUGHT THEM ALL THEY WANTED,
MORE THAN YOU CAN AFFORD
AND AN HOUR AFTER YOU GOT HOME,
THEY SAID....
TATTY WE ARE BORED!

   Why did the kids get bored an hour after they came home? How long do you think the kids should have been happy with their toys?

   ____

   ____

5. Can you think of a time when you really wanted something and you were sure that it would make you happy?
   How long did that happiness last?
   After you got it, did you realize that maybe it wasn't so important after all?

   ____

   ____

   ____

   ____

6. BUT KIDS WHO HAVE GOOD MIDDOS,
ARE SIMPLY NOT THAT WAY
THEY KNOW HOW TO APPRECIATE
WHATEVER COMES THEIR WAY.

   How could these kids have made their trip to the toy store more enjoyable for their father and for themselves?

   ____

   ____

   ____

   ____

7. I'D BE JUST AS HAPPY AS I WAS BEFORE
IF ONLY I'D LISTENED
AND TRUSTED YOU MORE,
I IGNORED YOUR ADVICE,
NOW I'M PAYING THE PRICE
I WENT WITH ALL OF MY KIDS
TO A STORE!

   What could the father have done to make this trip to the toy store a nicer experience for everyone?

   ____

   ____

   ____

   ____

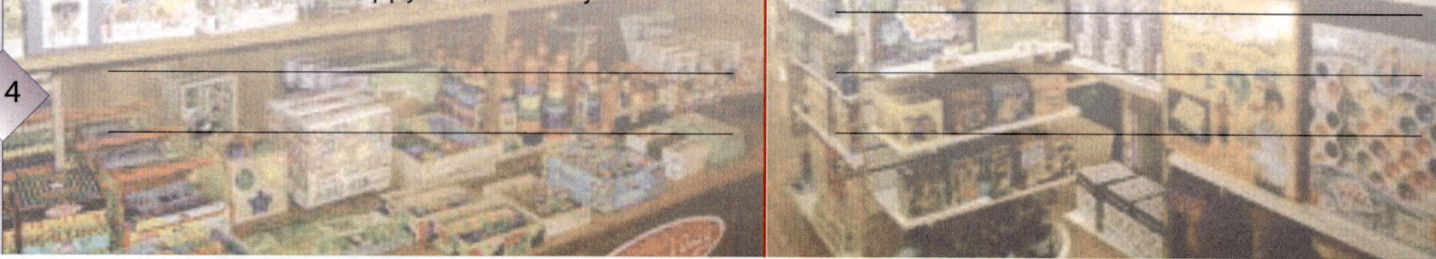

Let's Try That Again, Okay?

Expressing Your Needs Respectfully & Effectively

OUR FAMILY NEVER DOES ANYTHING FUN.

YOU NEVER BUY ME ANYTHING!

MOMMY, WHY CAN'T YOU BUY ME ONE? EVERYONE ELSE HAS ONE!

YOU PROMISED!

YOU LIKE MY BROTHER BETTER! HE HAS ONE, SO WHY CAN'T I?

Let's try this again.

What would be a nicer way to ask for what you need or want?

1. Make requests, not demands. Your tone of voice, the words you use, and your body language will make the difference between a polite conversation and an argument.
2. Offer to participate in some way, through your own money or effort. ("What if I help you in the garden?" "What if I use the birthday money from Grandma?")
3. Express your needs respectfully, without criticizing or accusing. Explain why it's important for you to have this. "It's important for me to have a knapsack with wheels because I have to go up a big hill." "I feel uncomfortable when I keep borrowing my friend's calculator in math class."
4. Stay away from YOU statements:
   "You said/You didn't/You always/You never/How come you/Only you… "
5. Find a time to ask that's not busy or stressful – DON'T ASK for things an hour before Shabbat, or when your mother or father is on the phone, etc.
6. Before you ask for something, think about whether you really need it. Don't ask for too many things at once.

In the following examples, how could kids communicate their needs more effectively?

☹ "BUT I NEED A NEW PAIR OF GOGGLES! EVERYONE ELSE HAS SPEEDO!"

☺ ______________________________

☹ "IT'S NOT FAIR! EVERY TIME WE GO ON A SCHOOL TRIP I HAVE TO COPY PICTURES FROM MY FRIENDS' CAMERAS BECAUSE MY CAMERA TAKES SUCH LOUSY PICTURES. WHY CAN'T YOU BUY ME A BETTER CAMERA?"

☺ ______________________________

☹ "YOU PROMISED US EXTRA RECESS! ALL THE OTHER TEACHERS LET THEIR CLASS STAY OUT AFTER THE BELL."

☺ ______________________________

The Thneed Syndrome

CREATING NEEDS & WANTS WHERE NONE EXISTED

How do people start needing things that they didn't need before?

1. **Technological advances**
   EXAMPLE: 100 years ago people didn't need telephones or washing machines.
2. **Rise in standard of living / social pressure**
   EXAMPLE: 100 years ago people had only one Shabbat outfit and one weekday outfit.

3. **Advertising**
   EXAMPLE: The De Beers diamond company coined the slogan "A diamond is forever" in 1947, turning diamonds into a symbol of engagement. Today, every kallah needs a diamond ring. It wasn't always this way!
4. **Affluence**
   EXAMPLE: When people have extra money to spend, they look for new things to spend it on, such as fancier vacations and more gourmet food, and eventually these things become needs.

Here's an illustration of how a need is created:

In a book called ***The Lorax***, by Dr. Seuss, a fellow opens a factory for a new type of garment called a "Thneed," and a creature named the Lorax ridicules him for creating this useless item.

To which the fellow responds:

"A Thneed's a fine something that all people need!
It's a shirt. It's a sock. It's a glove. It's a hat.
But it has other uses. Yes, far beyond that.
You can use it for carpets. For pillows! For sheets!
Or curtains! Or covers for bicycle seats!"

The Lorax said, "Sir! You are crazy with greed.
There is no one on earth
who would buy that fool Thneed!"
But the very next minute I proved he was wrong.
For, just at that minute, a chap came along,
and he thought that the Thneed I had knitted was great.
He happily bought it for three ninety-eight.

I laughed at the Lorax, "You poor [silly] guy!
You never can tell what some people will buy."

Can you think of any "Thneeds" that you have?

(i.e., items that have no real use or value but are considered important or essential)

UNIT 4

BUDGETING

Amusement Park Activity

Goal:

Learn to budget effectively using time as the unit of currency.

Instructions:

You and your friend have three hours (180 minutes) in an amusement park. There are 18 rides and attractions to choose from. (You can go on each ride more than once, if you choose.) How will you budget your time at the amusement park so that you can get the most out of your trip?

Ride/Attraction	Waiting Time (in minutes)	Ride Time (in minutes)	Total Time	Minutes used
1. Alpine slide	40	2	42	
2. Batting cages	5	5	10	
3. Boat ride	15	10	25	
4. Bumper cars	20	7	27	
5. Carousel (merry-go-round)	5	6	11	
6. Ferris wheel	10	8	18	
7. Flying swings	6	4	10	
8. Haunted house	25	5	30	
9. Junior roller coaster	5	4	9	
10. Loop-the-loop double upside-down backwards roller coaster	40	2	42	
11. Moonwalks	10	10	20	
12. Petting zoo	0	15	15	
13. Pirate ship	20	3	23	
14. Regular roller coaster	20	3	23	
15. Sky drop	25	1	26	
16. Tea cup spinning ride	20	3	23	
17. Train ride	5	12	17	
18. Water flume	30	5	35	
			Total:	

6 TIPS

for budgeting your time effectively:

1

You can do ***some*** of the things you want but ***not all*** of the things you want.

2

If you plan ahead of time, you are more likely to get to the rides you really want to go on. So decide at the beginning what's more important to you.

3

The rides/attractions that are more popular have a longer waiting time.

4

You can go on a few of the popular rides, or a lot of the less popular rides.

5

Just because a ride is popular doesn't mean that YOU will enjoy it. When deciding which rides to go on, think about what *you* like to do, not what everyone else says you *have* to go on.

6

You can't use even one minute more than you have (in this case, only 180 minutes).

6 TIPS
for budgeting your money effectively:

1
You can have some of the things you want but not all of the things you want. That means you will have to choose some cheaper items and some more expensive items.

2
If you plan well, you are more likely to get the types of supplies you really want. So decide at the beginning what's more important to you.

3
The items that people want more usually come at a higher cost.

4
You can get a few more expensive items, or a lot of cheaper items.

5
Just because a name brand is popular doesn't mean that YOU will like it. When deciding which items to buy, think about what *you* like to have, not what everyone else says you *have* to have.

6
You can't use even one penny more than you have.

Pack Your Knapsack:
Budgeting Activity

Goal:
To learn to budget your money effectively.

Instructions:
You are given $55 to spend on school supplies for the new year. Using the price list provided on the next page, choose which supplies you would like to purchase. Decide which items you want to buy in the "basic price" category, which you want to buy in the "medium price" category, and which you want to buy in the "high price" category.

Rules for this Activity:
1. You need to buy every item on the list.
2. You cannot spend a penny more than you have.
3. You are allowed to keep up to $2 of the money if you go under budget. The rest of the money needs to be used.

Item	Description	Cost
Crayons		
Eraser		
Folder		
Glue		
Looseleaf		
Markers		
Spiral notebook		
Pens		
Pencil case		
Lead pencils		
Ruler		
Scissors		
	TOTAL:	

Pack Your Knapsack: Budgeting Activity

Price List

Item	Basic Price (Rock-Bottom)	Manufacturer Name / Description	Medium Price (Middle-of-the-Road)	Manufacturer Name / Description	High Price (The Best)	Manufacturer Name / Description
Crayons	$1	No brand, 10 crayons	$3	Crayola 24 crayons	$8	Crayola 98 crayons with sharpener
Eraser	$0.50	Plain white	$1.50	Cartoon figure, bubble-gum smell	$3	Extra big with brush and case
Folder	$1	Standard, one-color	$3.50	Mead five-star	$7	Paul Frank with Julius the monkey
Glue	$1	Shoprite brand	$2	Elmer's school glue	$5	Sparkly Elmer's
Looseleaf	$3	Plain, no name	$8	Staples easy-open looseleaf with plastic front for inserting pictures	$20	Avery D-ring heavy-duty easy-to-open
Markers	$2	8 RoseArt markers	$6	10 Crayola markers	$13	24 highligher Sharpies
Spiral notebook	$1	Plain spiral, Walmart Great Value	$4	Mead five-star	$16	Juicy Couture
Pens	$2	Package of 6 plain ballpoint Bic pens	$4	Pilot G2 pens (6)	$8	10 gel pens
Pencil case	$4	Plain, one-color, one zipper	$8	All-zipper cute one	$15	Kipling with hanging monkey
Lead pencil	$1	Regular no-name lead pencil	$4	Bic #2 lead pencil	$8	Mechanical personalized lead pencil
Ruler	$0.50	Plastic short	$3	Sturdy, long metal	$7	Long, wooden ruler with built-in hole puncher
Scissors	$1	Small, not so sharp, good enough for paper	$3	Target standard school scissor	$9	Super sharp, easy-to-hold, fancy high-tech colors, blade-guard
Total	**$18.00**		**$50.00**		**$119.00**	

MESILA
Providing The Path to Financial Stability

UNIT 5

SOCIAL RESPONSI-BILITY

SOCIAL RESPONSIBILITY SCENARIOS

1a. A Real Bar Mitzvah - Part 1

Joey's parents want to make him a simple bar mitzvah. Some of Joey's friends have simple bar mitzvahs, and others have more lavish affairs. Joey wants a more lavish bar mitzvah. His parents offer that he can use the money that will come in as bar mitzvah gifts to upgrade to a fancier bar mitzvah. Joey is in a dilemma. Then, he goes to his friend Sauli's bar mitzvah, which is a really simple event. At that bar mitzvah, his other friend Meir looks around and says, "It just doesn't feel like a real bar mitzvah."

What do you think Joey decided?

Was there anything wrong with what Meir said? Don't we all speak that way sometimes? Do we realize the implications of our casual observations?

1b. A Real Bar Mitzvah - Part 2

Simon, who is sitting on the other side of Meir, whispers to Meir, "I think Joey might be having his bar mitzvah here too. You might have made him feel bad."

"What difference does it make to Joey?" Meir scoffs. "If this is where he's planning to have his bar mitzvah, he shouldn't care about what I say."

Meir doesn't realize the power he has. How would he feel if he knew that Joey used his own bar mitzvah money just to avoid Meir's disapproval?

2. A Pretzel By Any Other Name Tastes the Same

A big bag of pretzels costs $1.99 and contains enough snack for 10 recesses (20 cents each). Individual snack-size bags of the same pretzels costs $4.99 for a package of 10 (50 cents each). Moshe's mother bought the big bags of pretzels and gave them out to Moshe and his four brothers and sisters:

5 kids x 180 school days x 20 cents = $180 over the course of the school year (if you buy only the big bags)

5 kids x 180 school days x 50 cents = $450 over the course of the school year (if you buy only the individual packets)

That's a difference of $270 – just for morning recess!

If you were buying snacks, which ones would you buy? Could you see any reason why someone else might buy the other type?

Why isn't Moshe happy with the snacks he gets? What could Moshe's friends do to make him feel happier? What could Moshe tell himself to make himself happier?

3. In Fairness to Others

Mrs. Cohen goes shopping for a new backpack with her third-grader, Mark. Mark immediately chooses the most expensive, designer-label backpack in the store. There are another two backpacks that he also likes, but not as much. The fancy backpack is usually double the price of the others, but now it is on sale for only $15 more than the regular ones. Mrs. Cohen can afford it, but she tells Mark that she is not buying it.

"But Ma," Mark begs. "My friend Rubi just got that backpack!

Why doesn't Mrs. Cohen want to buy the more expensive backpack?

SOCIAL RESPONSIBILITY SCENARIOS cont'd

4. Check Out My Fancy Camera

Eli is going to Camp Achvah this summer and wants to make a good impression on his bunkmates. When he unpacks, he leaves his suitcase open on his bed just long enough for everyone in the bunk to see his brand new, top-of-the-line digital camera.

Why might this be unfair to the other boys in the bunk? Why might this be unfair to Eli?

5a. Less is More - Part 1

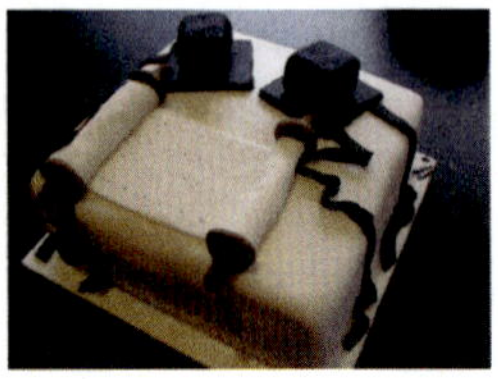

Simon saves up the money he earns running errands for the neighbor to buy nice bar-mitzvah presents for his friends. He really wants them to be happy, and he doesn't want to disappoint anyone. But he's finding himself working an awful lot just to keep up with all the bar-mitzvahs. Then, when his bar-mitzvah comes along, his friends chip in together to buy him a single, nice set of sefarim, at a much lower cost per boy.

How do you think Simon feels?

5b. Less is More - Part 2

Simon is thrilled with the gift, even though it only cost a few dollars. "I'm so relieved," he tells his mother. "I see that I don't have to buy such fancy presents to make my friends happy. Now I don't have to work so many hours."

In what way did Simon's friends give him a much bigger gift than just a bar-mitzvah present?

6. Backwards Compliment

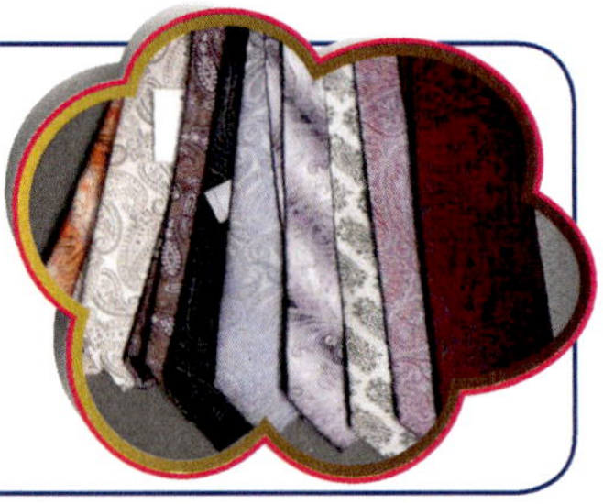

"Oh, I really like your tie!" David tells Jack. "I saw it on sale for $4.99 last week. I guess that's why the whole world has it!"

David meant to give Jack a compliment. How do you think Jack felt? Do you think he ever wore the tie again? What do you think he said to his mother when he came home?

7. The Shoes Have to Go

Victor's Shabbat shoes are three months old, still in fine condition but certainly not snazzy and new. Victor is going to sleep over at his friend Yoni's house for Shabbat and wants to look his absolute best. He looks at his Shabbat shoes and suddenly feels that they are completely unwearable and embarrassing. Last Shabbat, he thought they were just fine.

If you were Yoni, and you knew how he felt, what would you say to Victor?

8. Mister Popularity

Charlie just switched classes and he wants to make friends quickly. On his first day in the new class, he makes sure everyone sees his huge Rebbe sticker collection and costly school supplies.

To his surprise, at recess time, he notices that all the boys are crowding around Benny, whose clothes, knapsack, and coat are clearly hand-me-downs. Benny doesn't have any fancy albums to flaunt and he could use a new pair of shoes, Charlie thinks. "Why do they want to be friends with him?" Charlie wonders.

SOCIAL RESPONSIBILITY SCENARIOS cont'd

9. How to Ruin Someone's Day Fast

Isaac's father buys him a chinuch set of arba minim, which Isaac is very proud of – until his friend Shaul sidles over to him and asks, with a glint in his eye, "How much did that set cost?"

Under what circumstances would it be okay to ask someone how much something cost?

10a. Nothing to Eat - Part 1

In advance of the class trip, Rabbi Feldman, the teacher, announces that the boys should not bring any nosh or spending money on the trip. The school would give out snacks to everyone. During recess, the class was in an uproar. "That's so unfair," Gabriel protests to his friends. "What's wrong with bringing my own pocket money to buy what I want?"

Do you think all the kids in the class agree with Gabriel? How might the atmosphere on the bus be different if all the boys would enjoy the same nosh during the trip?

10b. Nothing to Eat - Part 2

Gabriel and a few other boys complain to Rabbi Feldman about the no-nosh, no-money rule.

"What if we don't like anything the school gives?" they ask. "We'll starve!" Rabbi Feldman grudgingly agrees that it's okay to bring a little nosh or a few dollars just in case. That evening, the supermarkets are packed with Rabbi Feldman's students, buying "a little" nosh and racking up a big bill. Describe some of the conversations that might have gone on after school that day in their homes.

11. Will the Best Bike Please Stand Up?

Jason and Abe are participating in a bikeathon to raise money for tzedakah. They know some kids have really cool bikes, and others have plainer bikes. Jason and Abe happen to have better bikes, but they decide to use their older brothers' secondhand bikes so that the kids who don't have nice bikes should feel better. When the conversation turns to how much the boys' bikes cost – "$100! $200! $300!"
Jason pipes up, "My bike was $10 at the flea market!"

Is anyone going to think less of Jason and Abe for showing up at the bikeathon with second-rate bikes?

12. Too Much Money, Right?

Morris and Eddie are going to Super AdventureLand on their Chol Hamoed trip. They ask their friend Ezra if he wants to come with them, and he says he has to ask his mother.
"My mother said we have other plans for today," he tells them.
"Oh," they say knowingly. "Is it too much money?"
Why was their question inappropriate? Is there any way Ezra could answer truthfully without disclosing information that he doesn't wish to disclose?

SOCIAL RESPONSIBILITY SCENARIOS cont'd

13. Please Don't Flip My Tie

Danny's mother buys him a new tie. Danny likes the tie a lot – until he flips it over and looks at the tag. "I can't wear a polyester tie!" he says. "The guys are going to make fun of me!"

"How can they possibly know?" his mother wonders. "It's a beautiful tie – you can't tell that it's not silk."

"But what if they decide to flip my tie and check?" Danny asks.

"I can't believe kids would do that," his mother says confidently. "But if you're worried, you can just cut out the tag."

"Then they'll for sure know it's polyester," Danny insists. "Trust me, I can't wear this tie."

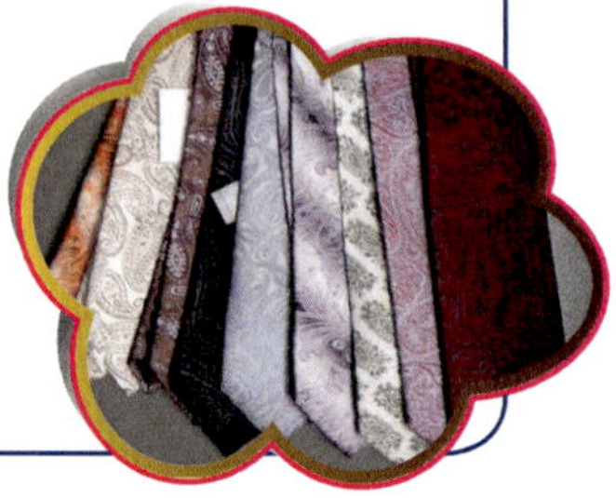

Is Danny being overly anxious? Is there anything wrong with a polyester tie? Why do some people need to know what other people's tags say (whether the tags say the brand name, price, fabric content, etc.)?

14. The Favor of Not Flaunting

"Uh, I can't study Monday night," says Ralph. "It's not going to work for me. I'm really sorry, Sammy."

Levi looks up at his brother Ralph, who is just hanging up the phone. "Why didn't you tell your friend that we go out to eat in a restaurant with Grandma and Grandpa every week?" he asks.

"I don't know if Sammy's family is able to go out to eat ever," Ralph says. "Why mention it?"

Would Sammy care if he knew that Ralph ate out with his grandparents every week?

How would Ralph's relationship with Sammy be different if Ralph would come into class every week and chat about what he ordered the night before at this week's fancy restaurant? If people would talk less about the things they have that other people might not have, what favor would they be doing?

15. Social Responsibility: Your Scenario

Choosing one of the four values listed below, think of a scenario (real or imagined) that would demonstrate the value. The scenario can highlight the value in either a positive or a negative manner.

1. **Positive peer pressure**
2. **Avoiding conspicuous consumption**
3. **Discretion and privacy**
4. **What you have is not what you are**

UNIT 6

BECOMING A SMART CONSUMER

Becoming a Smart Consumer

A Tale of TEN COFFEES

Has this ever happened to you? You take out your wallet, sure that it's going to be full – **but it's empty!** *Where did all the money go?* you wonder. Keeping track of the small stuff is challenging, but it can do wonders for your finances. Trivial purchases add up: 50 cents here, $2 here, and before you know it, that money from your grandparents is gone.

This happens to adults, too. **Let's take a look at one of the ways that people's pocket change disappears.**

Coffee Type	Price per Cup	Price per Week (1 cup a day)	Price per Year (1 cup a day)	Price per Year (3 coffee drinkers in the house, 1 coffee a day each)
1. Homemade, Folgers instant	$0.10	$0.70	$36.50	
2. Homemade, Taster's Choice instant	$0.16	$1.12	$58.40	
3. Homemade, Taster's Choice singles	$0.25	$1.75	$91.25	
4. Homemade, brewed in a Keurig with individual packages	$0.50	$3.50	$182.50	
5. Homemade, iced coffee	$0.60	$4.20	$219	
6. Convenience store, regular coffee	$1.75	$12.25	$638.75	
7. Coffee shop, iced coffee	$1.99	$13.93	$726.35	
8. Coffee shop, latte or cappucino	$3.49	$24.43	$1273.85	
9. Coffee shop, frappucino	$3.99	$27.93	$1,456.35	
10. Restaurant, gourmet	$6.25	$43.75	$2,281.25	

A Tale of TEN COFFEES

REVIEW

Answer the questions below using the table entitled "A Tale of Ten Coffees" on the previous page.

1. Fill in the prices in the column at the right.
2. How much money would someone save every day by going from a store-bought frappucino to a homemade Keurig brewed coffee?
3. Mrs. Azar drinks a Folger's instant coffee every day, including Shabbat and Sunday, and buys a latte during her lunch break when she's at work. She works five days a week. How much is she spending on coffee every week?
4. To raise money for their high school yearbook, Hanah and Sara sold iced coffee at the school production. They prepared about 100 cups of iced coffee and sold them for $1.75 each. What was their profit?

DISCUSSION

For his birthday, Mr. Brown's wife buys him an insulated coffee cup, and she starts preparing him a Taster's Choice instant coffee every morning for the road. "You know what?" he tells his wife. "This is just as good as the stuff I buy for $1.75 a day on my way to work! And it sure saves me a lot of time!"

Mr. Brown! You're not only saving time – you're saving a lot of money too!

1. If Mr. Brown buys coffee 5 days a week, 48 weeks a year (subtracting holidays, fast days, etc.), how much will he save every day by drinking the homemade coffee? ____________

   Every week? ____________ Every year? ____________
2. If you suddenly found yourself with the amount of money that the Browns are saving every year, what could you do with it?
   a. Which presents would you want to buy for the people you love? ____________
   b. What do you wish you had in your house that you could buy with that money? ____________
   c. What would you want to save up to buy? ____________
   d. Which tzedakah organization would you want to give the money to? ____________

Several years ago, the New York office of the Shuvu organization received a modest donation from a family in the Midwest USA. The donation was accompanied by a note:

> Our family is deeply impressed and inspired by Shuvu's outstanding work. For a long time, we have wanted to contribute, but have not had the means to do so. I am a rebbe, and our family's income is very modest. At a recent family meeting, my children calculated that if we would forgo soda on Shabbos for a year, we would be able to send you a donation. Our gift is enclosed.

Every penny adds up, as Chazal say:

פרוטה לפרוטה מצטרפת לחשבון גדול (סוטה ח:)

One small coin, together with other small coins, add up to a large sum.

Understanding Unit Cost

HAVE YOUR CAKE – AND PAY FOR IT, TOO!

Shmiel Schlemiel, the new yeshiva cook, decides to bake his very first chocolate cake for the boys. He takes his chocolate cake recipe out of his brand-new recipe box and takes it to the store as a shopping list:

This is what his store receipt said:

"What a ripoff!" Shmiel thinks.
"This cake is costing the Yeshiva $32!
I should have bought a fancy cream cake at the bakery down the block, for only $28!"

Shmiel, Shmiel, don't be such a Shlemiel!
This cake is not costing you $32!

Understanding Unit Cost

HAVE YOUR CAKE – AND PAY FOR IT, TOO! *(cont'd)*

Let's take a look at how much the ingredients for the cake will actually cost:

Ingredient	Price	Amount needed for recipe	Cost of amount used in recipe
A dozen eggs	$1.99	2 eggs	$0.33
5 lb. sugar	$3.99	2 cups sugar	$0.80
1/2 gallon oil	$6.49	½ cup oil	$0.40
1 jar instant coffee	$5.99	1½ teaspoons instant coffee	$0.15
1 bottle vanilla extract	$3.19	1 teaspoon vanilla extract	$0.06
5 lb. flour	$3.49	1¾ cups flour	$0.41
1 can cocoa	$3.89	¾ cup cocoa	$0.73
1 container baking powder	$1.79	2 teaspoons baking powder	$0.07
1 container baking soda	$1.49	1 teaspoon baking soda	$0.05
TOTAL:	**$32.31**		**$3.00**

ASSIGNMENT: PRICE IT!

Instructions: Every student, or pair of students, will take a recipe (minimum 6 ingredients) and calculate the cost of each ingredient, as well as the total cost of preparing the recipe at home. (For the sake of simplicity, the costs in this exercise are limited to ingredients.) Then, the students will determine the cost of buying the same product in a store or restaurant.

Note: If students wish to ask a storeowner or worker the price of a product that they have no intention of purchasing, they should explain their purpose in asking for the price, so as not to mislead the storeowner into thinking that they are actually interested in buying the item (which would be *onaat devarim*).

Optional: The students may actually prepare the recipe and share the results with the class, along with a detailed cost breakdown.

NAME OF RECIPE:

Ingredient	Price	Amount needed for recipe	Cost of amount used in recipe
TOTAL:			

SHOP LIKE A PRO!

Here are some tips for keeping costs down and making the most of your money:

1

If you're planning to buy a few items, make a shopping list. And stick to it!

Example: Harry went to the store planning to buy a pen and a notebook for school. When he spotted the new stickers on sale, he took a few packages off the shelf. When he got home, he discovered that he had spent twice as much as he had planned, on stuff that he didn't really want!

2

Pay attention to the various sizes available of the item you want. Larger packages are generally cheaper per item (assuming that you need the larger quantity).

Example: Max is buying cups for the class siyum. He can buy two packages of 12 cups for 99 cents each, or one package of 25 for $1.49.

3

Price the item you want in different stores. (You can just call them; you don't even have to go in.)

Example: Michael saved up his birthday money and Chanukah money until he had enough for the type of camera he wanted. He called six different stores and found that there was a range of $37 between the cheapest and the most expensive price – for the same camera model.

4

Generally, smaller stores (such as groceries) charge more than larger stores (such as supermarkets).

Example: Albert's mother sent him to buy a container of ice cream. At the corner grocery, it was priced at $8.49. At the supermarket it cost $5.69.

5

Stores stock basic items at the back of the store, and non-essential items in the front – or at the checkout counter – to get you to buy things you don't really need.

Example: Benny ran over to the store to pick up milk, bread, and eggs. Somehow, by the time he left the store, his bags also contained some chocolate bars and chewing gum that he had passed along the way.

SALE 6

A sale isn't a bargain unless you really need it.

Example: Avi was on line buying himself an ices for $1.75. The cashier told him, "If you buy five of those, they're on special for $5."
"But I only need one," Avi answered – and saved himself $3.25.

SALE 7

Don't shop when you're hungry.

Example: Dave stopped at a convenience store on his way home from yeshiva to buy some scotch tape. He was so famished, that when he spotted a bag of barbecue potato chips, he just picked it off the shelf and bought it. He didn't have much of an appetite for his mother's delicious supper when he came home.

SALE 8

Bring approximately the amount of money that you need, and not much more.

Example: Seymour is on a class trip with his friends. He wanted to bring along money to buy a cold drink, but he only had a $20 bill. After he bought his drink, and was left with a pocket full of change, he wandered into the souvenir shop and bought some gifts for his family. When he came home, he started wondering what in the world his parents would do with the stuffed lizard and "I ♥ NY" paperweight he had brought them.

SALE 9

If you buy the wrong thing, return or exchange it. Right away.

Example: After Joseph went off to yeshiva in Eretz Yisrael, his mother found a line-up of pants and jackets hanging in his closet, all with the tags still on. He had picked them up during his pre-flight shopping, but they turned out to be too snug on him… "Too bad it's too late to return this stuff," his mother mourned. "It's worth a fortune."

SALE 10

Count your change, and check your receipt for mistakes.

Example: Moshe bought a $2 flashlight for camp and paid with a $10 bill. It's a good thing he noticed that the cashier had given him four $1 bills instead of three $1 bills and one $5 bill. When he looked at his receipt, he saw that he had been charged $6 for the flashlight instead of $2.

MESILA
Providing The Path to Financial Stability

ACTIVITY

SHOP LIKE A PRO! MAD LIBS

ISAAC SAVED UP __________ (AMOUNT OF MONEY) FOR CAMP. HE WASN'T SURE EXACTLY WHAT HE WANTED, BUT HE THOUGHT THAT WHEN HE __________ (VERB ENDING IN -ED) TO THE STORE HE'D __________ (VERB) IT OUT. HE STUFFED ALL OF HIS SAVINGS INTO HIS __________ (NOUN), __________ (VERB, PAST) TO THE NEAREST STORE, AND __________ (VERB, PAST) UP AND DOWN THE AISLES, THROWING __________ (PLURAL NOUN) INTO A SHOPPING __________ (NOUN). "HEY, LOOK," HE THOUGHT __________ (ADVERB). "THEY HAVE __________ (NOUN) ON SALE. BUT ONLY IF YOU BUY __________ (NUMBER OVER 5). AND WHAT ABOUT THOSE __________ (PLURAL NOUN)? THEY LOOK __________ (ADJECTIVE)! IT'S A __________ (ADJECTIVE) DEAL! I'LL __________ (VERB) THEM OUT TO MY WHOLE BUNK!

ISAAC HANDED THE CASHIER ALL HIS MONEY, AND DIDN'T EVEN __________ (VERB) AT THE CHANGE. WHEN HE GOT HOME, HE REALIZED THAT HE HAD BOUGHT AN __________ (ADJECTIVE) PACKAGE OF __________ (PLURAL NOUN) BY MISTAKE. "I'LL EXCHANGE THIS WHEN I GET HOME FROM CAMP," HE THINKS __________ (ADVERB).

__________ (NAME OF BOY) ALSO SAVED UP __________ (AMOUNT OF MONEY) TO BUY __________ (ADJECTIVE) STUFF FOR CAMP. A __________ (AMOUNT OF TIME) BEFORE CAMP, HE __________ (VERB, PAST) DOWN ON A CHAIR AND MADE A LIST OF ALL THE THINGS HE WANTED: __________ (NOUN), __________ (NOUN), __________ (NOUN). HE PUT ON HIS __________ (ARTICLE OF CLOTHING) AND __________ (VERB, PAST) TO FOUR __________ (ADJECTIVE) STORES TO PRICE THE ITEMS HE WANTED. IN THE END, HE __________ (ADVERB) DECIDED TO BUY EVERYTHING IN THE __________ (ADJECTIVE) SUPERMARKET. WHEN HE WENT TO THE SUPERMARKET, HE BROUGHT ALONG A BIT MORE THAN HE THOUGHT HE'D NEED. HE NOTICED THAT __________ (ADJECTIVE) __________ (PLURAL NOUN) WAS ON SALE FOR ONLY __________ (PRICE). "WHO NEEDS THOSE?" HE THOUGHT. "WE HAVE PLENTY AT HOME." HE ALSO SPOTTED A __________ (NOUN) OF __________ (ADJECTIVE) MUSIC DISCS AT THE FRONT OF THE STORE BY HIS FAVORITE SINGER, __________ (NAME OF FAMOUS PERSON). "THAT'S NOT WHAT I SAVED UP FOR," HE SAID __________ (ADVERB). HE WAS __________ (ADVERB) PLEASED TO DISCOVER THAT HE STILL HAD __________ (AMOUNT OF MONEY) LEFT FOR THE CANTEEN BY THE TIME HE FINISHED HIS CAMP SHOPPING.

UNIT 7

RESPECTING PROPERTY

Yours, Ours & Theirs

Introduction

In order to manage your money, you have to know what's yours and what's not. If the boundaries between your property and other people's property are fuzzy, then you might unwittingly take or use things that belong to others, which is essentially stealing. Theft is not only about robbing a bank – it's also about using your friend's things without permission. And theft is not only about taking large amounts – taking a quarter without permission is also stealing.

We see the importance of working on honesty even in seemingly minor situations.

Basic Halachot of Integrity

In order to avoid any hint of theft, we need to know the basic *halachot* of dealing with other people's money and property:

1. You can't take things that are not yours without permission. That's called stealing.
2. You can't borrow things without permission. That's also called stealing. (Rambam, Hilchot Geneivah 1:2)
3. You can't hide or take away someone's things even as a joke. That's also stealing. (Rambam, Hilchot Geneivah 1:2)
4. If you borrow something, you have to return it on time. (Ketuvot 86a)
5. You can't borrow money if you don't know how you're going to pay it back. (Shulchan Aruch, Choshen Mishpat 97:4; Rabbeinu Yonah Avot 2:9)
6. You can't pressure someone to give or sell you something if they don't want to. (Rambam, Hilchot Gezeilah v'Aveidah, 1: 9,10)
7. If you find something that belongs to someone else, you have to return it.
8. If you can prevent damage to someone else's property, you are required to do so. (Rambam, Hilchot Gezeilah v'Aveidah 11:20)
9. It goes without saying that you are not allowed to damage, litter, or otherwise deface property, whether private or public. Damaging or misusing communal property is worse than damaging or misusing private property.
10. You can't waste or damage even your own belongings for no reason. (Sefer HaChinuch, Mitzvah 529 - *Bal tashchit.*)

It's the Little Things

Mar Zutra was staying at someone's house, and a silver cup went missing. When Mar Zutra saw a certain student wiping his hands in his friend's garment, he immediately announced, "He's the thief! For he doesn't care about his friend's money."

(Bava Metzia 24a)

Integrity Exercise

Instructions

Using the sheet entitled "Basic Halachot of Integrity," identify which halachah is applicable in each of the situations described below. Put the corresponding number (1-10) in the box following each situation.

Situations

1 Alan finds an expensive gold watch in shul. He brings it home and plans to put up signs to find the owner. But after Shabbat, he forgets all about it.

2 Sammy and Yaakov are in the pizza shop, and Yaakov is really in the mood of French fries. But his mother only gave him enough money for pizza, and he already spent his allowance for the next four weeks, as well as his birthday and Chanuka money. So he asks Sammy to lend him a few dollars even though he has no idea when and how he's going to pay him back.

3 Davie and Benny are in the same class. One day, Davie gets hungry, and spots an open bag of Bissli on Benny's desk. "I'll just take a handful," Davie thinks. "I'm sure Benny won't care."

4 Moshe lends David his Gemara notes two days before the test. "I'm planning to start studying tonight, so I'll need them back before school is over," Moshe says. "No problem," says David. "I'm photocopying them right now." But when David goes to the photocopy machine, he finds that it's broken. "I'll make copies tonight at the corner store," he thinks, "and I'll give Moshe his notes tomorrow. He doesn't really need to study today."

5 After Shelomo uses up all his canteen money during the second week of camp, he tells the canteen heads to write down how much he owes. "I'll figure something out," he assures them when they ask him when he plans to pay the large bill he has racked up.

6 The students find the gym closet unlocked, and they decide to use the equipment during recess. "We'll make sure to put everything back the way we found it," they tell each other.

7 David wants to use his sister Rachel's camera for his school trip, but Rachel doesn't want to lend it to him. So he pesters and nags until she finally says, "I'm sick of being nudged, just take it."

8 Teddy's going on a the train by himself for the first time, and he doesn't want to lose his money. He buys a new leather wallet and uses it for the trip, making sure to leave the tags on. The next day he returns it to the store and gets his money back. "It's in perfect condition," he thinks. "I was just borrowing it for the day."

9 The boys are at the pool in camp and they decide to hide their counselor Moshe's yarmulke and hat. Moshe comes out of the pool five minutes before Minchah, and all the boys think it's a riot that he has to go daven in a baseball cap.

10 Morris is almost finished collecting the stickers for the Shuls of the Universe album, but he's missing two that his neighbor Nissim has doubles of. He offers to trade Nissim four cards for those two, but Nissim says no. He then offers six, and eight, and ten, and eleven, but Nissim still refuses. But Morris is still not giving up.

11 Sammy's at a restaurant with his family, and he goes to the counter to take some ketchup packets. "These would be good for school," he thinks. He takes a bunch and stuffs them into his pockets.

12 Eliezer takes a bunch of children's books off his shelf and starts ripping out the pages, just for fun. "I don't need these silly books anymore," he says.

13 Ezra put his science project on his desk before he left the house. His brother Jack sees baby Charlie crawling up to the desk with sticky, chocolaty hands.

14 The kids on Maple Street decide to make their own Lag Ba'omer bonfire. "It's easy to get wood," they say. "We'll just chop down some branches from trees on the street. They don't belong to anyone."

15 The *minhag* in Camp Sunshine is to engrave your name somewhere in camp at the end of the season. Michael chooses the underside of the top bunk bed for that noble purpose, carefully inscribing "The great Mike was here" right above the spot he stared at from his bottom bunk all summer.

16 Solomon is walking down his block when he notices that the lights are on in Mr. Cohen's car. He considers knocking on Mr. Cohen's door to tell him, so that his battery shouldn't die, but he's in a hurry, and he decides that it's not really his business.

17 There's a big recycling bin for plastic bottles, and the kids managed to open it and get all the bottles to go rolling out.

רַבִּי יוֹסֵי אוֹמֵר,
יְהִי מָמוֹן חֲבֵרְךָ
חָבִיב עָלֶיךָ כְּשֶׁלָּךְ.
(אבות ב:יב)

Rabbi Yosi says:
Your friend's money should be as dear to you as your own.
(Avot 2:12)

Respecting Property
Yours, Ours & Theirs

Objective

To visually depict areas in which respect for property needs strengthening.

Rationale

Often, people are not sufficiently mindful of their responsibility towards property, whether their own, someone else's, or the community's. The root causes of this behavior can be one of the following factors, or a combination:

- Carelessness
- Lack of integrity
- Lack of awareness or knowledge

Instructions

Every student, pair, or group will identify a particular area in which respect for property needs strengthening, and will design a visual exhibit illustrating the problematic behavior and depicting halachically acceptable alternatives.

The exhibit should demonstrate creativity and knowledge, and should have a practical message for its viewers.

Possible Topics

- Respect for shuls, yeshivot, and schools
- Wasteful or destructive behavior
- Respect for parents' money and property
- Respect for friends' money and property
- Misusing public property (parks, greenery, signs, etc.)
- Integrity with money
- Subtle forms of theft or dishonesty
- Jokes & pranks
- Responsible borrowing
- Returning lost objects

This can also be done as a class project for creating community awareness, or as a class newspaper.

UNIT 8

ADVERTISING

MESILA
Providing The Path to Financial Stability

How Advertisers PLAY With Your Mind

Advertisers use many different techniques in order to get you to buy their product. Here are some of the common ways they play with your mind:

Are supplies really limited? Or is this just a way to get you to the store, quick?

1 Unsubstantiated or Unprovable Claims

Promises that sound good,
But can't be proven.

"Lowest prices anywhere."

"You won't find another house like this."

"Best ketchup."

"For skin like peaches and cream, use MagnaLotion."

2 Unfinished Claims

Claims that sound good, but mean nothing because they are not finished. They use words like less, reduced, lower-priced, or faster, better, cleaner, more, etc.

"UltraClean gives y ou more." More what?

"You can be sure if it's Westinghouse." Sure of what?

3 Guarantees

Advertisers try to make you think they're guaranteeing something, but that's not necessarily the case.

"Best photos. Guaranteed."

"Guaranteed to last."

4 Weasel Words*

A weasel word is one that appears meaningful at first glance but actually means nothing.

"Leaves dishes virtually spotless."

(Virtually makes you think that it's spotless. But they didn't say that the dishes are actually going to be spotless.)

"Helps control dandruff." (The claim is not "stops dandruff.")

5 Free Stuff

Everyone likes to get something for nothing. But if you're paying for their product, it's not a free gift.

6 Buy One – Get Something "Free"

"Buy a burger – get free fries."

---

* The expression "weasel word" is named for the weasel's habit of sucking out the inside of an egg, leaving it hollow but appearing intact. Weasel words, therefore, appear to be making a meaningful claim, but actually say nothing. Here are some commonly used weasel words: "helps"; "virtually"; "almost like"; "can be"; "up to"; "as much as"; "refreshes"; "comforts"; "tackles"; "fights"; "strengthens"; "the feel of"; "looks like."

How Advertisers PLAY With Your Mind Cont'd 1

7 Buy One – Get a Discount

You feel like you're getting something extra, but when you do the math, it's not as good as it sounds.

"Buy one – get 25% off the second."
"Buy three – get one free."

8 You Deserve It

Why do you deserve what they want you to buy?
And if you deserve it, why should you pay for it?

"You deserve a new dining room set."

9 Follow the Crowd

People like to belong and be part of the crowd.

"Everyone's drinking it – why aren't you?"

10 Stand Out From the Crowd

People also like to stand out and feel unique.

"Be different – do it your own way."

11 Rhetorical Questions

Advertisers ask you questions, leading your mind to come up with the answer they want.

"Shouldn't your family be drinking Hawaiian Punch?"
"Plymouth – isn't that the kind of car America wants?"

12 Catchy Slogans

Nothing like a good jingle or catchy phrase to stick in your mind and create a connection to a product or company.

"Coke. It's the Real Thing."
"Got milk?"

13 It's Good for You

Advertisers try to convince you that their product is good for you so that you'll feel that buying their product is the right thing to do.

"For heart health, go with our twelve-grain bread."
"Joe's Gym. Just what the doctor ordered."

14 Snob Appeal

Advertisers want you to feel special and "upper class" if you have their product.

"For people with good taste."
"SuperCool shampoo: For those who are a cut above."

15 Plain Folks

Some advertisements try to give you a comfortable, down-to-earth feeling.

"For people like you and me."

How Advertisers PLAY With Your Mind Cont'd 2

16 Scientific Evidence

By quoting statistics and medical or other scientific research, companies convince you that their product is effective.

"Proven clinical results."
"Studies show that Royal Paper Towels are 25% more absorbent."
"The headache medicine doctors recommend most."

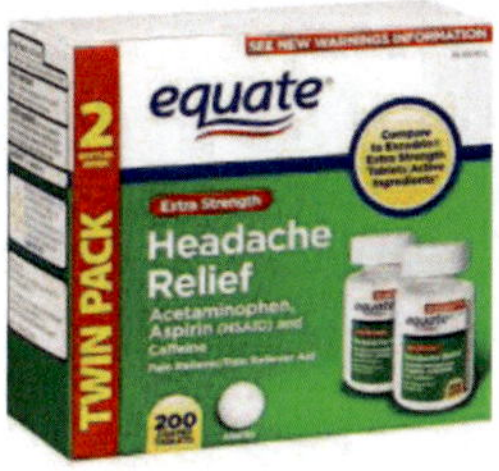

17 Celebrity Endorsement

Advertisers try to convince you that if a famous person has one, then you should too.

18 Brand Loyalty and Designer Labels

Designers labels make you think there's something special about a particular brand. Companies try to get you to develop a preference for their brand and a positive association with their logo and packaging. They want you to be their friends.

POLO
RALPH LAUREN

19 Tradition & Family Values

Companies want to convince you that they are more trustworthy and valuable because they have been around for a long time, and they try to give you a warm, homey, family-like feeling.

"Family owned and operated since 1956."
"Where tradition and quality meet."

20 Feel-Good Experience

Advertisers try to get you to associate a particular product with a thrilling or otherwise positive experience.

"It's the next best thing to being there."
"Everest Furniture Polish – for that rugged mountain clean."

MESILA
Providing The Path to Financial Stability

Activity:
How Advertisers Play With Your Mind

Part One

Below is an array of Coke ads.

Which ads are more likely to make you spend money you hadn't planned on spending? Rate them in order of appeal and effectiveness.

Part Two

Do It Yourself!

Choose a popular food and create an advertisement or series of advertisements promoting this food. The advertisements can include text, visual, audio, or a combination. Use at least one advertising technique or marketing strategy on the "How Advertisers Play With Your Mind" worksheet. How many techniques can you use?

Made in United States
Orlando, FL
04 November 2026

90201133R00038